T0094675

Sitcom
DAVID MCGIMPSEY

Coach House Books | Toronto

  Canada

Published with the generous assistance of the Canada Council for
the Arts and the Ontario Arts Council. Coach House also
acknowledges the support of the Government of Canada through
the Book Publishing Industry Development Program.

LIBRARY AND ARCHIVES CANADA CATALOGUING IN PUBLICATION

McGimpsey, David, date
Sitcom / David McGimpsey. – 1st ed.

Poems.
ISBN 978-1-55245-188-5

I. Title.

PS8575.G48S58 2007   C811'.54   C2007-904809-9

for Samantha

Foreword

Reba only slightly depresses me
Steve Urkel has seen me well past blue
Evan Drake stings like a nest of scorpions
Mr. Furley stirs up poison mushroom stew

Maude's voice haunted me into my teens
Chandler's a stuck tick of embarrassment
Deb destroys each molecule of resolve
Flo slaps me with a wet, bony hand

Lucy only slightly depresses me
Hawkeye is like being laughed at by girls
Uncle Jesse is worse than eczema
Jethrine's just eczema at the ankles

Gilligan reminds it's foolish to try
Jan Brady combs her hair a thousand times
Newman gets me running in small circles
Fonzie's a kind of sweet formaldehyde

Porky only slightly depresses me
Molly Dodd really doesn't understand
Rerun gets my nervous tic a-twitching
Roz makes me pour with a liberal hand

Gladys Kravitz undermines my ambition
Kate and Allie are a vague stink in my sheets
Buddy texts me the message 'Hello failure'
Bailey Quarters takes off her glasses and pukes

Marcia only slightly depresses me
Meathead asks, 'How do you spell *melancholy?*'
Schneider elbows me off coffee shop stages
Georgette sings 'Steam Heat' just to make me cry

Eddie's blog calls me 'Bonghog' and 'Pillsy'
Mr. Ed warms up the spoon while singing
Lassie tsk-tsks, 'I'm just disappointed'
Flipper straight out gives pistol-whippings

Tootie only slightly depresses me
Natalie had me wear homemade ponchos
Jo told me to stay away from L.A.
Blair told me to forget about Toronto

Holly went for drinks with me at Chez Jay's
Val smoked with me outside the Smog Cutter
Tina tried her best at Jumbo's Clown Room
Lauren went beer for beer at the Joker

Potsie only slightly depresses me
Skippy is pretty much off my compass
Boner saw me through six years on the couch
Cockroach yawns and says, 'You're a disgrace'

Kimmy Gibbler asks, 'Are you mental?'
Jenny Piccalo asks, 'Why'd you say that?'
Ethel says, 'You're your own worst enemy!'
Rhoda says, 'Are you saying I look fat?'

Princess only slightly depresses me
Sabrina took me out in '98
Kelly Bundy inspired my dreary sonnets
Kelly Bundy stabbed at my fingertips

Little Ricky just kept taking from me
Cousin Oliver just kept taking from me
Andrew Keaton just kept taking from me
Timmy Martin just kept taking from me

Daphne only slightly depresses me
Mrs. Naugatuck took my love of life
Mrs. G. gave me a D in ethics
Hazel said, 'Where'd Kelly leave that knife?'

Colonel Crittendon had a good left hook
Sgt. Carter a respectable kick
Inspector Luger punched right to the face
Major Dad lunged straight towards the neck

Jeannie only slightly depresses me
Barbara Jean taught me love does not stay
Ginger Grant said, 'I think we need to talk'
Agent 99 had to get away

Murray Slaughter sharpened the Ginsu
Keith Partridge performs sweet lobotomies
Ralph and Alice are like heart and disease
Reba only slightly depresses me

– D.M., Los Angeles, 2007

Act I

'Timon will to the woods'
           – *Timon of Athens*, 4.1.35

Invitation

Please join me on the occasion of my
thirty-ninth birthday. Drinks will be served,
esp. the mixed ones that announce
lounge-weary sophistication: *old-fashioned*,
lime rickey, *chocolate dancer* – though I only
drink Schlitz Light. Gifts are not necessary,
but should you be strolling downtown and see
some nicely framed limited-edition print
of a sad battlefield where a general's
caprice cost thousands of lives, or a pair
of antique binoculars, or a vintage
board game where the *Happy Days* characters
have to rush Fonzie to the hospital,
knock yourself out. Even a mail-order
certificate that allows me to perform
wedding services in the Philippines
would be a nice touch; but no funny cards
about aging, please, no *To My Friend*
on His One Hundredth Birthday, No You're Not
Just Getting Older … You're Losing Hair Too!
And even if you have bought me a ticket
overseas and secured a seat for me
at the finest hash bar in Amsterdam,
don't even *think* of saying, 'Welcome
to the Netherlands.' There will be hors d'oeuvres,
the tiniest of tiny foods, tasty
miniatures of already miniature snacks,
baby corn so small it'll look like Niblets,
taquitos so small, so *diminudo*,
they will be called *taquitoitos* and
they will look like the bits at the bottom

of a bag of corn chips. I also have hot salsa
I once bought in South Texas, on a dare,
which claims to use pepper-spray extracts
squeezed from the used big-nozzle canisters
of riot squads that have subdued the world's
most determined hippies – *drink up, my friends!*
There'll be a piñata made up to look
like an old college professor who once
predicted I'd go far, his hands in his pockets,
the pink-tissued face making him look like
a cartoon pig who sells insurance.
I can hardly wait to give that thing a whack.
Conversation's the most important thing
to me, you know, and I want to hear all
about your trips to Barcelona, your
remodelled homes 'not far from the city,'
the radio quizzes that you gamely won,
and all about the tipsy, week-long
adventures that involve the bronzed thighs
of lovers old and new. You need not censor
yourself from questionable phrases
such as 'bony pony' or 'nipple burn.'
I live for those stories but, FYI,
I have instructed many friends to steer
away from the following potentially
harassing topics: old hairstyles, jokes picked
from Dave or Jay, that time I thought *flammable*
and *inflammable* meant different things,
the summer I said I would 'concentrate
on my portfolio' and ended up
taking extra shifts at a frozen-yogurt stand,
enduring a long season of conversations
that were all *fro-yo this* and *fro-yo that.*

Let's not talk about those heartfelt novels
that try to adduce the spirit of a dead
father, novels period, pyramid schemes
and most things that stink of the eighties.
So, the music will be lighter on eighties
nostalgia than many of these gatherings
tend to be, but my mixed tapes will astonish
you with their blend of intemperate jug
bands, wounded young princes on their brand new
Stratocasters, logo-savvy DJs
flowing trip-hop bright beat jungle, Hawaiian
slack-key guitarists who are so laid-back
they make Rastafarians sound like aerobics
instructors. There'll be celebrations of
Gabrielle Destroismaisons, who's known as
'the French Britney Spears,' and Lorie,
who's also known as 'the French Britney Spears.'
Don't worry, if you get a strong desire
to hear 'a little ditty 'bout Jack and Diane'
we'll see what we can do. It's all going
to go smoothly, there should be enough space
for your coats and shoes in my little room,
and I hired a Portuguese interpreter
just so I could tell the person who lives
below me there'll be no need this time to call
the cops; *muito pesaroso*, dancing
will have to be done in your stocking feet
as the linoleum in my place scuffs
quite easily. If it gets late and I start
singing along to Mariah Carey's
'Never Too Far,' do not get embarrassed,
just let me go for the high notes and, as
a rule, assume all sexual confusions

are your own. Do not be surprised if, by
sheer miracle, my beloved should accept
my invitation and show up at my door;
you will no doubt be awed by her fine glow,
by a bone structure that is right now
waking Rodin from the dead, by a voice
you will stop to listen to, as if it were
about to reveal a secret you've been searching
for since you turned thirteen. My beloved
will then lead us all in a heartfelt round
of 'Happy Birthday,' and we'll share cake! –
coconut pillow divine – and stories
of past anniversaries where we'd turn out
the lights, dabble with the leftovers in
the medicine cabinet, lie on the sofa
and play a whole year's tape of phone messages.
If, unexpectedly, I excuse myself
from the party and walk into the cold air,
even forgetting a jacket, you can
rest assured I will not be gone for long,
no matter how tempting it would be
to go see a movie uptown, alone.
I would never think of abandoning
the beauty of your friendship. *Répondez*,
and, please, BYOB, just to be safe.

Reunion

What is my news? Well, since graduating,
I've raked it in and I've tossed it off,
I've plucked the green peach and sodded the pitch.
That is, aside from noticing the moon
shimmering on saw-bladed ferns in redwood
groves, I have learned two valuable lessons:
always floss, and nobody wants to see
your collection of shot glasses. Mercy.
I did not cry when Henry Blake died, though
I died every time Kinch deferred to LeBeau.
'That is so *you*!' I'm sure we'll hear that: 'You
were locked up nine months for passing bad cheques?
That is so *you*!' Of course, my high school band
never made the big time, never backed up
Thin Lizzy on their 'Boys are Back!' bus tour.
Maybe our band name, Wee Willie Nelson,
doomed us and I regret insisting on it,
regret writing it in Magic Marker
on the ass of my best acid-wash jeans.
I enrolled at Buford Business College
and just let the cocktails do the talking,
left the academy under green clouds
of vodka slosh and ended up working
on the busy side of the phone: 'But, sir,
your agreement says you should pay us now.'
Today, I supervise a fleet of young
phone hawks in both technique and bafflegab.
Admiral, that is just so you. Romance
came around for me more frequently
than Ernest movies and, alas, was almost
as annoying. There was Becky Plover

(do you know if she'll be reunioning?)
who wrote poetry about fast horses
and father figures in undershirts.
It was a miracle she was with me,
always pressing for what she called 'the truth,'
as long as the truth never again involved
a story that ends 'whacking off with Hazmat
mitts.' Who knew she'd serialize novels
about the hot hot sexual awakenings
of Toronto: 'She kissed his smooth tanned chest
and felt free.' O my asthmatic princess,
wringing your hands, your knock-off purse full
of neatly printed scheduled coffee dates.
Then there was salty Kathleen, who thrived
on confrontation, who grew with each
'piss off!,' who sprawled on rank sofas
and drank Pepsi while sitting in the tub.
Thank God she won't be there! I can see her
coming through the gym doors like a tank
through the palace gates in Saigon, flying
high on her own mix of Jägermeister
and milk, screaming, 'Where is that stupid fag?'
And, finally, Pamela, who I used
to love but who now says she has to try
to work things out with her husband. I asked
and she just laughed, saying, 'I really love
reunions, except for the part about
murder being a crime.' That is so her.
'It's been so long,' they'll say before turning
to say, 'It feels like only yesterday.'
My father thought the best way to fight
heart disease was to simply ignore it,
my sister yelling about his yellow pills.

I'm not so sure his approach wasn't wise;
my mother sits patiently by herself,
makes her own tea, her own little cheese plate,
and still laughs when a TV ad begins
'Do you have diarrhea?' Through the years,
while the economy boomed and bulldozed,
while computers made life much easier
for secretaries and Jar Jar fans alike,
while doctors fought AIDS and cancer of the neck;
while populations across the globe soared
and citizen geeks fought to save marshland
and limit greenhouse gasses for the sake
of the dooming tear in the ozone, while
geneticists promised the dawn of the clone
and the Hubble Telescope took pictures
of galaxies that folded neatly into
other galaxies, I took time to perfect
the art of the bummed smoke, the hindered dream,
the delayed comeback zinger, the late lunch,
the jealous funk, the revenge fuck, hollow
vows, saggy jowls, long happy hours,
debit cards, loose-fitting pants, nighttime soaps
(don't bring up the past), the hyena's laugh,
blaming it all on nice people like you.
That was me in your medicine cabinet.
That was me hanging up just as you picked
up the phone. What's the theme of the reunion?
'Always and Forever: This is Us!' or
'May God save us from more remakes of
Planet of the Apes?' It'll just turn out
everybody's all dressed nice, showing off
how our spouses taught us not to say 'nothink.'
Spruced from long apprenticeships in the malls

and cubicles since we left sweet Hoodlum High,
we know how to deny the neighbourhood.
Good guys all, we'll hear, all shy and quiet,
nerds and geeks who forgive the only school
in the state to be closed due to 'benzene
poisoning.' We'll transform *poor* to *cute-poor* –
cartoon-Brooklyn poor or Rydell High poor.
Will there be awards? I'd like to see that.
Can I put my name up for Most Improved
Sense of Persecution? Naturally,
the award for Most Exactly Where We
All Thought They'd Be has to go to Charlie
G., who smashed his Chevette into a pole.
Would I see that guy – you know, the guy I once
punched in the stomach for five delinquent
dollars – get up, fight the piercing feedback
of the microphone, accept his lame prize
as Nicest Guy, and weep for 'the best times
of our lives'? I'm sure Nicey's all set up:
probably doing lines off a whore's thigh
while the whore's tax attorneys look on.
I will be at the reunion. I will dance
to T'Pau and I will do impressions
of old teachers 'til they pry me off the bar.
But there will come a time when it gets dark.
The lights against the wall will hypnotize.
In frosted mirrors behind the Pernod
I will see couples dancing and realize,
for me, partying's no different than waiting
for a late flight out of Newark: despite
the sequined dress of yearned-for Sasha-May,
despite the welcoming handshakes, I opt
for the vampire who lives behind the wall;

he has leather chairs and a rifle range,
a pet tiger he likes to call Earl,
a desk into which to carve the words *It's over.*
Alone, I'll smell the factories again
and retrace the steps to the shops of my youth,
where they sold candy made out of petroleum
and just one brand of soft, gleaming white bread.
I'll see shiny elbows on my sport coat
and, just like that, all attendees will seem
like fat rich kids on ponies. They never ask
if the pony's back is sore, they only
say, 'I wanna lollipop!' Wouldn't it
be great if the nicest girl, and I mean
the most legendary Jesus-Loves-Me queen,
showed up all divorced and brandy-weary?
And if we excused ourselves to some long-lost
stoner's enclosure made for bra-strap
fiddling, and we'd satirize everything,
including Sasha-May, including my
own dreams of a *one-off* and, looking in
her green eyes I'd say, 'We better get back,'
just as the band returned to play 'Footloose.'
'I thought that was more of an encore,'
I'd say, tucking my shirt into my belt,
and sensing our shared booby-prize despair,
she'd take my hand and gently remind:
'Koo-Koo, the nice thing about crawling
into the woodwork is staying there.'

Dinklihood

What is there to do but solder wires
and listen again to *Pink Diggly Diggly*?
What is there to do but admit I'm tired
and move to the west side of East Smelly?
Should you find the ghost of Natalie Wood
would you recommend my earthly boner?
Should I lose all to a European bid
will you not call me the Prince of Posers?
One's value is not just social pride,
which I should always try to remember
when seated by a laminated sign
that explains the Heimlich Manoeuvre.
Drink up, Pasquale, I have an abscess;
drink up, Dingus, I have scalped your tickets.

Architeuthis

'A good student will always learn to laugh
at old professors,' Dr. Miracle
wrote on my paper about *Dorian Gray*.
I had no idea I'd ever be
on the other side of his maxim
and I regret making fun of how he'd say,
'Now, let's dive into the wild that is Wilde.'
I wouldn't have taken that shady job
teaching writing at the local college
if I didn't have innate confidence
my VCR could tape afternoon soap operas.
Coming home to refrigerator pudding
and envelopes I'd slip into the trash,
I loved the way soapers slammed gin tumblers
and how monologues weren't botched
with impertinent interruptions.
'Jeremy, I'm leaving you,' Lainie would say,
and Jeremy would look on like a fat seal
as she finished her *I'm so sorry* sentence.
I marked papers the way Dr. Miracle did:
with flinty, sarcastic remarks in red pen.
The first class I ever taught was on Ibsen's
Hedda Gabler. I paced the room, punchy,
and my real teaching 'career' started when,
frustrated with my hedging, one kid asked,
'Don't you think Hedda's a total bitch?'
I did not roar out of graduate school
and wait in the halls of the MLA;
I gave up on finding that teaching job –
much like Emilio Estevez
gave up on making hit motion pictures,

or the way Ray Parker Jr. gave up
on dominating the Billboard Top Ten –
and I doddered sessional to sessional.
Once, when I still believed in stepping stones,
I had to teach an Intro to Lit class,
absurdly early in the morning
to kids who wanted to be dental
hygienists. They would just look at me
and sneer, 'With teeth like that, what could
you teach us?' I never talked to the guy
I shared my office with – he was worried
I'd light up one of the cigars that sat
on the corner of my desk. Once, a student
came to see me while I was working
on a jigsaw puzzle of Aquaman –
she never mentioned it, but through our talk,
you could tell it was on her mind.
Dr. Miracle would have been appalled,
even if he spent much of his spare time
studying legends of the giant squid
while decanting his favourite spirits.
'Architeuthis,' he would say, 'is no myth.
One hardy restaurant on Canal Street
tried to cook a three-foot-wide suction cup.'
When I told him I was writing poetry
he set for me this simple exercise:
'Write four rhyming couplets, if you can,
about four different squid (save *architeuthis*).
You may have to go to the library.
The couplets should say something factual
about the natural state of the squid,
that most misunderstood of species.'
Loligo forbesi is what we like to batter,

Found in most seas of Atlantic waters. .
The opalescent squid's white as a ghost
Found mostly off the California coast.
Loligo vulgaris depends on weather:
It shrinks and grows with the temperature.
The Caribbean Reef squid lives beneath all light
Its large side fins are as large as kites.
'Nonsense!' he wrote. 'But good amateur verse!'
In one of the soaps I watch, Ryland,
the wastrel son of Thomas Pressleton,
swims free from a town car, run off
into the ocean by Houghton Canning,
who was to marry Ryland's true love,
Amy Summerland. Ryland fights his way
to the suburban wedding ceremony.
Dripping wet, he screams, 'Amy! Amy!'
Now, I find it hard to return phone calls
and I brush off requests from a lawyer.
My students often come to talk to me,
sensing I'm a washed-up outsider
and I might have something to say besides
'I can only judge you by your work.'
I don't. I'm one bad day away from *fuck off*.
I have my own problems being loved;
what could I tell General Gabler's daughter?
How can I sink without sounding like
I was the saga's tough cap'n, like
Leontes assuring, 'Let us be clear'd
of being tyrannous' before sending
Hermione to her unkind death?
Weekends, I'm entranced by a Richard
Simmons infomercial where the greased-up
star sidles up to desperate fatties

who have lost *hundreds* of pounds with his help.
He'll ask things like 'What was Evelyn like
on the inside?' and he'll hold her thinned hands
while she speaks of herself in the third person.
'Evelyn was lonely, near dead inside.'
He's like Mother Theresa for the fat,
the St. Jude of the morbidly obese.
I knew two-minute meals and twelve-hour shames;
oh, how could I tell Dr. Miracle my
hero was no strange squid or Oscar Wilde
but a five-hundred-pound oaf in a half-hour ad?
I lived just above a late-night gyro stand
in an apartment with mice and a neighbour
who just loved to play the opening licks
to 'Over the Hills and Far Away.'
I saw the end of life: the Ventolin,
the monitoring of high-blood-pressure pills,
the little TV in the semi-private
room. Students say they never watch what's on,
not even the buoying love of Ryland,
shaking off a lily pad in the aisle.
I did not think of how it would work out,
never took the time to remind how
their students would learn to laugh at them.

Opera

Down to his too-tight track pants, the tenor
is more or less what you would expect.
Esp. if you expect the kind of guy
whose greatest moment was killing a pimp
in *Grand Theft Auto*. He's well over forty,
and when he's on the couch yelling at the likes
of Richard Hatch, Sanjaya and Ralph Malph,
he's not killing time before batik class
or even waiting to drive to the West End's
Nymph Garden Mall. He sings 'Lucky Love'
but loses his breath and has to take a nap.
When he gets up, sofa cushions are kicked
like field goals, and he wails, 'I win, bastard!
Bastardo, I have won! I, Bat Bastardly!'
A baritone, the best friend, still in work clothes,
mouthful of Cheezies, starts reciting
his passive-aggressive *recitativo*:
'What d'you want to do? Wherever you want
to go that's cool with me … as long as
it's not a bar, restaurant or the movies.'
Upstage, the tenor phones the baritone
and they talk about the important things:
the rigours of springtime Scotchgarding,
the spread between the Ravens and the Jets,
and a largely fabricated memoir
that takes place at the Huff Dormitory
and involves one of the future stars
of *Grey's Anatomy* and three-buck wine.
An action-setting duet moves downstage:
deep in a tavern with a nautical theme,
the tenor suggests the way ice gathers

on the stairs up to his apartment simply
'destroys him.' The baritone waits for a pause
between arias and says, 'Have you noticed
how country music these days sounds more like
Bon Jovi than Merle Haggard?'
The baritone has made this point before.
He's said it to his parole officer
and whoever mans the phones on the show
Wake Up, Grimshaw County! A new curtain,
a second act, where the love theme's advanced,
and the soprano (certain love interest)
and mezzo-soprano have detailed duets,
finishing each other's compliments: 'Your hair – '
' – looks amazing in this colour, I know!' 'Your ass – '
' – looks sexy in jeans, I know!' 'Your reading – '
' – of Fukuyama is preposterously
sentimental, I know!' They nibble
on steak sandwiches and sing about
this book where, it seems, two women are, also,
best friends: *The Sisterhood of Light Lunches*
at Fashionable Mid-Priced Restos.
The rest of the second act is set,
strangely, in an Atlanta tiki bar,
and the whole thing is mostly the tenor
singing about whether he should order
a mai tai or a sufferin' bastard.
God, you know rum. Tell me which way to go.
Remind me again of Hawaii Five-O;
affirm with me, O Lord, the thing to do
is sit back, put up my hand and order two!
The orchestration becomes uncertain,
piccolo and clarinet pairings sputter
and another curtain falls as a bassoon

makes a sound that is not encouraging.
The third and last act seems concerned with death,
or, at least, the tenor is assembling a coffin.
By large windows that overlook restless
St. Petersburg, Florida, the tenor
works away. A month ago he was to make
sweet Beeline-novel love to the soprano
but, sidetracked by crushes and binges,
he defends his decision to refuse
a job at a reputable mid-sized
firm that finances tax-reform campaigns.
The tenor planes at the coffin's edges
gently, then calmly waxes and shines
as if it were an antique surfboard dinged-up
by the great Duke Kahanamoku.
He sings of ships bound for Cyprus at dawn
and, closer to home, of glorious college days
and the even more glorious days
of quitting college just to play basketball
every day in a noon pick-up league
with guys who had names like Big Ugly Jim,
Hook-Shot Guy and Big Ugly Considine.
The sopranos do not *bel canto* the air
of the third act. A previous libretto
had the mezzo, a good girl from the 'burbs,
ask the tenor if he'd ever been in love.
She was to listen to his strange response,
touch him and say, 'We all hide something.'
It was all edited out in deference
to a new ending, which had everyone
moving to Ajax, but it's *interesting*.
He was to say he'd never been in love
but, holding a kitchen knife, shamefully

reveal he came close to loving a fembot
built in a basement labratory
by Miraculo, *basso profundo* –
Miraculo could not fool the tenor.

14 Episodes

Joey discovers a chimp wearing pants.
Joey tells Sara he believes in Jesus Christ.
Joey tells Sara he 'overstated' his faith.
Joey's sister Gina considers death.
Gina calls Sara 'too superficial.'
Gina discovers Joey's secret stash.
Gina and Sara go a bit too far.
Gina tells Joey the chimp has cancer.
Sara pretends to be a Scottish nurse.
Sara and Joey's romance hits a snag.
Sara judges a super-hunk pageant.
Sara thinks Joey is going to hell.
Joey prays for the soul of Sir Chimpy.
Joey tells Gina he's found a new hope.

Snap

Her sisters used an acne soap called Snap,
a tubbed, gritty mess which sat like a puck
and washed like a thousand jagged rocks –
the kind of soap refinery workers used
before punching out and heading for home.
It smelled like wet sand and sour aftershave
but her sisters swore nothing worked better.
So, when the pimples first pimpled over
she scrubbed her face raw every night
and she loved it, she loved it, she loved it.
Soon enough her pillows and T-shirts
took on the scent of medicated Snap,
and she no longer wanted to go hang out
by the wall behind Perry's Corner Store,
no longer sat to watch *The Rockford Files*
with her perpetually stoned brother.
She wrote her first song, 'Pink Hearse Rehearsal,'
pledging 'loyalty to death and to pills,
loyalty to the greenness of our gills.'
Thank you, Snap: with a fishy red face,
she took to the world outside school
where blue-collar men tried to sing like Cher
and old-school junkies golfed like Sam Snead.
She met the keyboards and the rhythm guitar,
and, soon enough, the pages of a plucky zine
became her pineapple-faced devotional.
The zine was mostly her lyrics and drawings:
images of wolves and grey handguns.
She cut her hair right over the sink
and hung out in bars like a regular.
It was in Earl's Bar or the Bandicoot

where she scribbled the lyrics to her song,
'My Father's Killed Better Horses Than Me.'
People in the city still know that song.
She rarely saw her brother anymore,
wouldn't talk to her sisters on the phone;
sitting in her apartment, drunk to Jupiter.
There was a band called the Mentalo Five
of which she was supposed to be a fifth,
but she rarely made it to rehearsals.
She plucked out songs about the grip of death,
about the need to be alone, and a spoof
about Jesus Christ coming back to earth
just to enter a chili cook-off:
O Lord, you may be the sweet son of God
but your five-alarm chili is for pussies.
With bottles to lighten and pipes to light,
she kept her eyes towards her floorboards.
Used to not looking at pictures or mirrors,
used to arrangements with ten-dollar crooks,
pimples sprouting like mushrooms near her eyes.
Grey, finally working some Jennifer's job,
searching old pillboxes, new vodka flavours,
a hopeful Cézanne agenda-planner
which had only one determined entry:
'Paulie, what do you say we just get high?'
O, just a little Virginia creeper
and just a smidgen of trumpet vine;
a healthy bushel of mayapple
and a wicker basket of jessamine.
Another promise to God that she'll be good,
a gentle saint by all intentions,
at least until her spotty spotty face
finds the bar at 29th and 2nd.

Is she breathing? Has she greened out her gills?
Goodbye goodbye. Goodbye Jack, goodbye Jill.
She bought it, took it and weighed her options,
letting go while thinking up inventions:
the edible mop, the springform rock,
the resealable Hershey's kiss, kiwi twists,
the grey unitard, the mortal Mallomar,
the evader, the last inhaler, Snap.

B– / C+

This is a most interesting paper,
David. You have a rare sympathy
for both Osric and Arthur Carlson –
intriguingly placed in the middle
of your paper on W. H. Auden.
Auden undoubtedly read Shakespeare
(though that quote you employ on page 7,
'Viley Shakey is drooping mambotastica,'
should not be attributed to Auden,
or any poor poet, for that matter).
And maybe Auden had a take on *Hamlet*
that stretched to its scene-stealing fop,
but it is most likely he did not,
as you suggest on page 12,
'sympathize deeply with the quaint argot
of Les Nessman.' W. H. Auden
sadly died in 1973,
a full five glorious years before
WKRP *in Cincinnati* aired.
How would he have known Les from Jennifer?
Johnny Fever from John Caravella?
Besides the obvious anachronism
(and I'm not sure you're not just being droll)
there was a liveliness to your writing,
even if it wasn't, as you say, 'academical.'
In fact, many of the things you say strike me
as original. One of the few times
you actually came to class you said
Timon of Athens was an unreadable play
about 'a fucktard who has a hissy fit
when he realizes he can't buy friendship.'
Though preposterously obscene, I thought

yours was the best reading I heard in class.
So, again, I was roused reading your takes
and I wasn't taking the mid-paper nap
that is standard in my grading regimen.
Maybe it's best not to impeach myself
reminding you the Spanish Civil War wasn't
fought over 'Iberian Stamp Taxing,'
and Medieval Denmark was not noted
for 'its painful shoes made from cockles.'
I won't harp on typos or grammatical slips,
on your penchant for calling the Moderns
'the prophets of "that's a pretty big *if* "'
because you remind me of a young me.
Just last month, I was high on Vicodin
(I mean, I was calling the TV Mommy;
I mean, I was hugging my shoes like children;
I mean, the disembodied head of ALF
was floating in my kitchen saying, 'I love you
as much as I love the fancy mustards.'),
judging stories in a local contest –
all these homey tales of curious cats
and unhappy couples in their apartments ...
I wasn't grossed out by the bad writing,
but, in my fog, appalled with myself,
I thought, *Who am I to judge anything?*
Was I any less naive when I set up
my shelves in my little office at Buford
Business College? I was a lucky puck.
My colleagues told me my hiring was a fluke
but I smiled like a fleet banjo player.
In their eyes I was just a bald barber,
funny around a comb, loved about town.
As good as any nine-fingered butcher,
laughed at, a palpable Herb Tarlek,

mixing plaid with plaid in a swell of jeans.
Like Osric, I'm here to remind Hamlet
the king's wagered 'six Barbary horses,'
like Arthur Carlson, to stammer assurance
that the station-format change to 'all rock,'
Mother, is completely out of my hands.
So, David, I dream of the same thing you do
and you know who I mean: she sits up front
and laughs when I bring up my theatre days:
the humiliations of auditions,
learning life lessons while in full dress.
But I'd never ask her to Mexico;
she'd assuredly miss her great home state –
the one with all the granite quarries,
the one where she pines for young men like you
who'll treat her poorly and be on their way.
So, don't wake up the dean, little Arthur;
I bet you Uncle Ben had to listen
to endless stories about cooking rice,
probably sometimes wondered, 'How come
nobody ever asks me about potatoes?'
Is it any different out there for you?
Isn't your favourite episode predictable?
The one where live turkeys are dropped
from a helicopter? I bet anything:
my collection of ceramic ibises,
my copy of Stevens' *Harmonium*
annotated by a young Jim Varney,
my autographed picture of Susan Hawk.
A gleeless cog, I can't give you an A
when you say Auden, to 'pay for a wig,
sold tremens-inducing diet pills to kids.'
These comments may not lead to graduate school,
but, David, you will always have a friend.

CanPo

O, bubbly seal, why do you collect leaves?
Do you know how I promised my mother
I'd take her to see the Ice Capades?
Don't cry for me, my sweet Shatner,
it's just you and me (and maybe Shatner).
Don't you know I told most of my students
how happy I am to be a poct?
So happy! I'm almost in heaven
and I'm throwing Mardi Gras beads
to Elisha Cuthbert and there's confession
in the morning. O, something-something loon,
do you think I could ever forget
the greatest people in the whole country:
the Tampa Bay Buccaneers' grounds crew?

Timon

Let me put away the videotapes
that once surrounded my Ikea desk.
May Mary Tyler Moore snarl vindictively
as I confess I am powerless against
those ads for Axe deodorant.
I am powerless over OxyContin
but I am esp. powerless
over those ads for Axe deodorant.
It's just like a bath in Hai Karate
followed by a shower in Aqua Velva.
But long before such odorous assurance,
showing the kind of sober foresight
that guides a porn star in a tattoo parlour,
I decided it would be best if I went
after my Ph.D. I was gamely intructed
by old school dons tougher than Kojak
whose resumés sounded as impressive
as the credits to a PBS series:
the words 'foundation' and 'endowment'
resonating quite nicely alongside
the usual ring-a-ding of 'Harvard,'
'Princeton' and 'chair.' Soon, I was teaching
on an adjunct contract at TBU
and, Cletus, I threw the most awesome parties.
I let my students tap kegs they rolled
out from my own expansive keg cellar.
I was convinced that I had it all:
my poems were read at pancake breakfasts
and solved the ancient poetic question,
'What if Virgil was Screech on *Saved by the Bell*?'
Perhaps 'solved' is a little too strong.

Let's just say I took a strange little turn
when it became clear I was not loved
beyond the miracles of keg-tapping.
Sweet Keggy Keggleson could take me
to her pasture in Old Keglahoma
and I would know what was on her mind
and it would definitely not be me,
and not just because I'm old as radio.
Didn't Kegs write mash notes to her teachers?
'Professor Kindness, thanks for the calming
touches on the shoulder as you passed by;
O, Dr. Sensitive, thanks for the copy
of your own annotated *Theogony*.'
Those were the kinds of profs who never failed
to call you stupid for taking Tae Bo.
For the great sin of loving Kelly Clarkson
they'd make you carry Ronald Reagan's bags,
even though you're used to carrying things
in your own *Tuff Li'l Gipper* roll-away.
I kept my mouth shut! One helpful colleague
patiently defined 'euphemism' for me,
concerned I might think it a shampoo brand,
and I never said aught but 'That makes sense'
when I could have said, 'It's like how "tipsy"
is euphemistic for "parlously drunk"
which itself is a choice euphemism
for "I asked your wife to go to Paris
with me and she leaned in and suggested
the Knight's Inn off Exit 3A."' Nimrods!
From hence, regents, grad students and alums:
I hope all your lawns are filled with pudding
and not even a flavour you sort of like.
You could tell me TBU's medical school

invented a pill that cures both despair
and jock itch, and I would not return there.
May TBU be swept up in rashes
and the most horrific cases of bedhead.
May it know the chafing a bus driver
knows. Alone, I no longer need a TV
or the special-edition DVDs.
I know the episodes of *Mr. Ed*,
the timeless sitcom about a talking horse,
like the back of Ed's hoof. The one where Ed
dreams he's a studly soap opera doctor,
making all the housewives swoon,
or where Ed becomes a Lincolnphile
and attempts to free all the caged birds
in Los Angeles. Who better than me
to ask the undemanding walls:
I can understand Ed loving Lincoln
and how he would see Lincoln's policies
extending to the animal kingdom,
but where did Ed get the horse-sized long coat
and the horse-sized stovepipe hat? Amen.
On my tombstone, may it just be written:
Here lies he who loved freedom, of course,
as much as he loved a good talking horse.
No need to ask God to take it all away
when, eventually, it all goes away.

Act II.i

'And does the old wound shudder open? Shall
I nurse again my days to a girl's sight,
Feeling the bandaged and unique night
Slide?'

– John Berryman, 'Sonnet #39'

Precious

Precious as the love between a man
and either Betty or Veronica,
sweet as spending the night in a van
with a bottle of no-name Goldschläger.
Into the thicket the gnatcatchers go,
grey winged with high-pitched mating calls;
I take you to my parents' bungalow
after three Big Macs at the East Side Mall.
Sweet as toffee muffin without the muffin,
gentle as a less-howly howler monkey,
soft as soft-serve, cute as a postcard puffin
riding the back of a ceramic donkey.
Mom's on meth and Dad's left for Vancouver,
so let's skip school and love one another.

Absolution

It is absolute: Mary Ann or Ginger?
The pain comes in having to make a choice,
when Love knows both Ms. Summers' 'quince cobbler'
and Ms. Grant's turn in *Los Angeles Nights*.
The choice may seem less known or understood
when someone in a bar laughs at your jokes.
But soon enough it stands in front of you
like a schoolyard brute who asks, 'Face or gut?'
When she shows you photos of her children,
when she says, 'We have to talk' over the phone,
you know how to answer the question:
Not-Ginger, I take thee; *Not-Mary Ann*, I do.
Not-she knows your castaway fantasies,
laughs when you say you choose to be happy.

Susan #42

'Apemantus's intentions in *Timon*
are not clear,' Dr. M.'s tangent brownly
began. Maybe he saw some of himself
in the poet-cynic role and he looked
about the room as if he'd long given up
on the prospect of actual listening.
It was never much fun in his class.
Dr. M. tugged at his frayed jacket cuffs.
Maybe he was being 'Athenian,'
in his way. His evals used other words.
Susan did not know of the trouble play,
though she knew this story about some guy
who lived for four months in a multiplex:
he said his favourite film was *Breakdancin'*
and that he still likes movie-house popcorn.
Poetry workshop had never been fun,
particularly as it was non-credit,
and now Susan, who sat right up front,
was to have her pieces critiqued in class.
Susan wrote: *A tiger's spots always change*
A noodle's white biscuit always flowers
A dancer's black harness always ponies
And they call the wind Metadonna.
There was not much time left for the poems;
by the time Dr. M. finished his defence
of cynicism as 'perhaps the only
spiritual value worth having,' Susan
got to hear only a few stray comments.
Replying to her poem, Dr. M. wrote:
'This is daffy material, worthy
of one of your newspaper columns.'

She wrote for a magazine – not the paper.
Next meeting, wearing the exact same suit,
Dr. M.'s puffed-up dramatic reading
of the *paragone* scene (where painter
and poet duke it out to see who's the boss)
in *Timon of Athens* was ridiculous
but there was time for Susan's rival, Todd.
Todd wrote for the same city magazine,
and took the course, he said, 'to scam chicks,'
but something else was really going on.
Ever since being buried in a Reno
snowstorm, Todd was writing out his life:
the hokey relationship he once kept
with the folkie hotbod who kept guitars
near the bed and who'd sing requests
as Todd fell asleep; a Scrabble rodeo
in Seattle where the word 'dominos,'
e-less but acceptable, won the day;
long afternoons arrested in a despair
that confused friendship with Thai massage
and hope with a sale at Ralph's Liquor Barn,
a despair that seemed to poke holes in his eyes,
walking through the city, waiting on love,
walking through the city, realizing
if somebody stopped to say, 'Hey!
Nice shirt!' he would have to always love
the shirt-appreciator, and he would write
116 shirt-lover sonnets
just to do one more than Berryman,
who did just one more than Shakespeare.
I'd scorn to exchange my shirt at Sears.
'If I ever see Reno,' Todd asked God
as the Donner Pass snows kept falling,

'I won't ask for more. I will know death
like a bracing shot the bride's father pours
and I will open books and learn a few words
from a dead language to chase it down:
I ask you, Dear Lord, how long must I wait
to slip in a box two by two and by eight,
maplewood stained to a fine commonplace
agus fagaimid siud mar ata se.'
In class, Todd's poems were more transparent.
Living for today is just not my thing.
What good is today if you won't call?
He read it and paused there as if it hurt
to expose himself in such a manner.
Betting on unhappiness had been my life:
I looked for love from those who could not give.
I'd write a hundred poems and just laugh,
It's not like I don't know I'm off to the grave.
Your smile is sweet, you curl up like a pea,
There are silences I can't breech or regret.
Living for today is just not my thing.
What good is today if you won't call?
At some pokey coffee shop after class,
there was lots of love for Toddy. Susan,
with espresso, wished them new strains of flu
and muttered something about twenty-nine
dollars a class. Poetry was a scam too,
a rich kid's way of arranging respect,
a second car parked by a bungalow.
Susan knew Todd, knew him to seduce interns
by composing teen-weepy homilies
to 'friendship,' when the only friendly thing
they'd done was give each other mohawks
after too amply Long-Islanding

their iced teas. 'I will to the woods,' Susan
said as she got up, while Todd made time
with a pretty girl whose awkward poems
were obsessed with 'haunting hospital smells.'
Was she the little pea in Todd's poem?
Was that the kind of poem that appears
in a prestigious journal like *Tearsea*?
At home, a little TV and a lot of
You have NO new messages in this mailbox,
she ups-and-downed herself in the mirror
for an unhappy half-hour and then wrote
a poem she called 'The Vase and The Jar':
The vase shades the jar with precocious grey
and the grey covers an air force of boys
in crewcuts from quaint midwestern towns
who destroy every single hot inch of Spain.
Susan's sure the poem answers her critics
but, like someone staring at a new lesion,
she's conscious of sad fate. Episodes end,
heartaches become anecdotes and poems,
once 'glib and slipp'ry creatures,' are dragged
to the trashcan icon on the bottom right.
Living for today is just not my thing.
What good is today if you won't call?
Susan prepares for a new love interest:
straight-talking Kenny 'The Hammer' Fleming,
a hockey goon sent down to the minors
for once daring to try to score a goal.

Guelphadelphia

Did I not protest love to a college girl?
That wintry intersection across town,
where I also understood the snow swirls
could not hide she thought I was a gorgon.
She was as kind as anyone from Guelph,
averse to words like 'ugly' or 'assface,'
but it came together in wet winter
when she said, 'Let's not even be *buddies*.'
Considering she didn't know Buddy Ebsen
and quoted lines from *Sex and the City*,
it was pretty easy to not be her friend.
But still, spring came on most slowly.
Some girls just purse their collagen'd lips.
Some girls just want to talk fake tits.

Vicki

The musky musks of the Regal Beagle
faded in the fibres of your white pants.
You had stopped counting *Die Hard* sequels
and my promises to give you a real chance.
How can I explain the L.A. hotels,
the spirited conversations about menus
('The tzatziki's fresher! The figs are lyrical!'),
and my faith in 'So, what do you want to do?'
And that's the extent of my rationale,
in someone's tub in Venice, drunk to hell.
You did karaoke. What did you sing?
Your cranberry-lime-flavoured herpes cream
was left on the dash of my Jeep Cherokee.
Don't you know my wife looks through my things?

Susan #43

'Dave Schultz's cruel beating of Dale Rolfe,'
Kenny tells Susan, 'opened up my eyes
to hockey's beauty and what it means
to be Canadian.' A behind-the-net
pounding, you retain the right to bleed,
puddle yourself into the dread tropes
of Southern Ontario: stubby ales,
Syl Apps, and sitting on a train ride
with a wispy Methodist minister
who can predict the dismal lengths of winter
from leeward peeling on paper birches
and take three strokes off your golf game.
Susan reads Kenny the Goon as mistake,
a sexualized maternal instinct,
an outgrowable affliction with a stick.
She compares Canada to senior year,
to a face full of nasty girl-acne,
'a nation of sorority pledges'
always crying for the unringing phone,
humourless poets, inept suicides,
still pretending to know how to speak French.
'Oyez! Schultz's beating of Rolfe is relief
from all that Can-crud and means I'm free:
free to the Ford Pintos and Ford Escorts,
free to Haylie Duff or Hilary Duff,
free to be cuckoo for Cocoa Puffs,
to leave the soul-saving to the preachers.'
Kenny, for his philosophical part,
joined, 'Forgetting the new rules to hockey
and slashing someone who called you *assface*
is wrong, but, still, c'mon, a minor offence,
like skipping confession for the movies

or telling a girl you'll call her back soon.'
Susan takes umbrage at this, his comments
about phones. She didn't listen to the rest.
Said she'd written seventeen 'harsh' columns
about how men promise and don't call back,
how it's caused women more grief than high heels,
football season and Tyra Banks combined.
Even contemplating the great snow geese
who sacrificed so much for her pillow,
Susan is unable to fall asleep. She writes,
still keeping notes about an office rival,
thin-hipped/grey skirt/straightened hair/fastest track
and, nervous, she wakes up Slashy Kenny
and asks him to write a list of ten things
he thinks are special about her. 'Special,
you know, things that are unforgettable
and please, Kenny,' she pleads, most serenely,
'no gratuitous use of the word *booty*.'
Did Schultzie ever have it so? Next week,
on team stationary, well out of town,
the Goon had his considered *love ya* list:
– A polka-dot dress the same colour scheme
as Crest toothpaste, loose about your shoulders.
– That crepe-paper thingy in the bedroom.
What the hell is that? What the hell is that?
– Did I not protest love to a college girl?
The one with the goony step, chubby cheeks
and hair she herself permed to poodle curls
which would take seven weeks to unkink.
I've never been good at picking up clues
but I've been good at looking idiotic;
I can't love you like my poodle-topped boo,
but I am keen on what they call 'the sex.'
Pancake ass, why must you make such a fuss

when it all could have been so easy?
I would have settled for a text message
saying HOSS I THINK U R THE SHIZZY.
Hey, did you check out titostacos.com?
You really should, it's totally awesome!
Susan crumples the paper in her hand
and decides to give Bud Light a chance.
Susan says she knew Kenny wouldn't stay,
not long enough to discover her point –
they're both living out their childhood dreams,
but strange, unknowable versions of them.
Would it be better to hang up the skates
and work at Quiznos rather than be Schultz?
Wouldn't it be better to bake sourdough
than string out one's teen penchant for writing
by churning out peppy magazine columns
chock-a-block with cab drivers' quotations?
Fucking Canadians. Susan's so good
at rejecting the very things she wants most,
thinking a European man should skate
towards her, smiling in a way that reveals
the crags in his eyes. Susan knows something,
knows something about death, how death finds you,
even in America, sure as Schultz finds Rolfe;
even if your arms are stretched wide open
towards the Pacific, in surrender,
even if you're admitting you don't know
much about love. It's not to cry or lose sleep;
alone, she hears pigeons nesting in the eaves
and all throughout the nooks of her building.
Kenny appears in her dreams, cooing:
I will skate back there and I will punch out
your boss-slash-unresponsive-lover tonight.

Turn-ons

When Love's in a liberated city
and has a room with moderate rates,
what kind of amusement would Love select?
What kind of pornography would Love read?
Glossy hardcore fare all pink and white?
Or a Playmate from East Iowa State,
raising her skirt towards the vast plains
from a window in the school library?
Love's turn-ons include: mind-reading, ice cream,
making grand apologies for simple faults.
Turn-offs include: pushy people, the D word,
and (of course) unmentholated cigarettes.
Tell me, within the city's teeming throng
does Love spend me-time shopping for thongs?

Capri

Laura's wearing two-piece pyjamas,
pretending to sleep under the covers
even though they now sleep in separate beds.
Laura's wearing a tight black knit sweater,
a pleated tweed skirt with houndstooth checks,
telling him what he needs is a lawyer.
Laura's wearing a white vinyl raincoat,
double-breasted and with inch-wide buttons
which she does not do up but holds together,
modestly, with her right hand. With her left
she shoos him away – the way a cop would.
Laura steps out wearing a tight black dress,
no earrings or bracelets, but a mink stole
which catches his nose as she swings it around.

Wicked

She had stomach problems. It made peeking
into her medicine cabinet less fun
than it should be. Her thick beige syrups
and chevron-shaped pills would scare anyone.
The intricate dance of her real sickness –
a cross-pollination of stress (she claimed)
and 'trace glutamate,' a wheat protein –
was less impressive, coming across like
the unnamed malady of a talented
but troubled student who'd doodle pictures
of genies' lamps instead of answering
exam questions. Her apartment was warm,
well furnished and full of pristine, trendy
accoutrements: vanilla soap, glazed tiles,
plush Bloomingdale's towels, imported rugs
and a noiseless dehumidifier.
Bookish, too, each room with maplewood shelves
stocked heavily in trade non-fiction:
Fatal Chic: The Electronic Alley;
Schenectady Dream: Inventing Edison;
One Hand Clapping: Staging the Trouble Plays;
Pared Apples and Corkscrew Tracheotomies:
The True Story of the Swiss Army Knife;
Advancing Through the Impartial Darkness:
The Poetry of Rebecca Plover;
Thomas Buford: The Majestic Beauty
of Discount Higher Education.
Not a place where a man who was used to
sleeping in his clothes could feel really free,
but I was dead grateful for the invite.
Since quitting a job I had at Kinko's

I'd been singing in a local café
called Ludica for the generous bits
in a passed-around hat. Her kindness
was directed towards a homemade soup
which she stirred as she talked on and on.
A soup full of gourmet-grocer things:
fish and sausage, chick pea and okra –
smoky, spicy, nothing she'd ever eat.
I took spoonfuls of her soupy tonic,
which she took pleasure in serving to me
as if I were her boy. I was hungry,
I savoured and listened to her go on.
She said, 'When dumb people try to sound smart
is when they'll say the dumbest things.
The books dumb people always overpraise
are kind of like the fancy sitting rooms
of a new immigrant's house. I mean, like,
is there, you know, anything tackier
than the rooms they consider fanciest?
You know, the plastic-covered sofas?
The china figurines of boys peeing?'
Soup-bound, unsure what she was trying to say,
I did not defend my Aunt Katherine's
collection of tea cozies, boxed neatly
in a glass curio my Uncle Jim
spent six cheques on. I stayed with the soup.
Suddenly, she was putting on her coat,
saying, 'I know just what this soup needs!'
and she bounded off like a cheery elf,
the door banging shut before I was sure
she was serious. I stayed with the soup.
I waited for an hour and a half.
She didn't have TV, so I was reduced

to browsing through *Spectral Erotics:*
The Lover in the Late Romantic Age,
and fell asleep on her quilt-covered bed,
which smelled like applewood and cardamom.
When the phone rang I did not hesitate.
A girl's voice called me by name, saying,
'You don't know me, but I'm Adie.' Adie
was the best friend, and she was with her.
She'd fallen sick again – maybe wheat flour
residue on the soup's garbanzos.
'She's sitting on the curb now, chilling out,'
Adie said, but not to worry. 'This stuff
happens all the time.' I asked, 'Where are you
now?' and she said they were at Zabar's
which I said was 'wicked' because I like
the word, it was so summer-in-Boston
sounding. I invited Adie to my next
coffee shop show and I 'hoped to see her there.'
'Are you asking me out on some date?
While your friend is puking on the West Side?'
I said, 'Not really,' but she still described
herself and her dislikes while her friend groaned
in the background. I was absurdly full.
The next time I played a Ludica show
I took to swearing in my onstage patter,
just to get attention. I imagined Adie
in the crowd, her hands ready to clap,
her vibrant spirit most noticeable
when she requested her favourite song.

Ginger

Did Elvis really love Ginger Alden?
The comely former Miss Traffic Safety
would sneak away from the out-of-it E
just to spend time with her normal boyfriend.
But, then, why speculate about Ginger?
She was just someone slow to get out of bed,
the first beauty queen to see Elvis dead;
who but God knows what her intentions were?
Elvis's love overwhelmed its object:
obdurateness must have seemed glorious
to a man determined to kill himself,
despite gold-plated pistols and private jets.
E found a good high in his new love and all:
Placidyl, Valmids and Demerol.

Crosstown

'In the end,' you said, 'it was just too hard
to remember your phone number.' Stingers
like that don't come along every day, not
even to a man who'd wear a beard of bees,
not to a man who'd sport wasps in his
corduroy pants after changing his name to
Captain Stinger. On the bus out, I wrote
down so-long poems in a spiral-bound,
dollar-store notebook. Like any creative
writing student would, I compared you first
to an abandoned bird 'twittering grief,'
and then, with a vengeance, to your mother,
right down to the 'talon-like fingernails'
and your magical ability to make
men disappear. Then I got into it:
Don't ask me to grow up and consider
the legion of lanky sperm donors
who'd queue up just for a shot with you.
You can Facebook with those dorks any day.
Self-conscious about the poetry, suspicious
all bus-riders like to peek, I gave up
and just sketched a professional-looking
bell-curve graph – a masterplot pitch
for a steamy, shirts-off *roman à clef*:
A) Like Heathcliff and Cathy ice-skating,
I really should read that book one day;
B) Somewhere in the middle, the girl
accustoms herself to the hero's smile
and his arrogant sanctimonies;
C) the girl looks completely ridiculous
in Banana Republic jeans, probably

in love with some Warren at the workplace
and Warren's read some of *Wuthering Heights*
as well as *Marjorie Morningstar.*
Furthermore, when Warren's asked if he's read
Marjorie Morningstar or *Middlemarch*
Warren never says, 'Are you fucking nuts?'
Out of the neighbourhood, the bus stopped
for a long time outside St. Teresa's.
Worshippers needed assistance to board.
I gave up my seat, but two high-schoolers
jumped into it, one on the other's lap,
their faces pink with a druggy Wednesday.
I wondered if I would ever have to plead
to St. Teresa? Would she be on my side
or yours? Did you ever consider
'the mystical spear of divine love,'
or were you always pretty much satisfied
with oversize sweaters and the songs
of Sarah McLachlan? The bus rumbled past
my stop but, still feeling stung, I stayed on
and continued to a part of town
I'd never seen, an area where most
stores sold utility meats or secondhand
shoes. That's where I want to live one day.
In a local tavern called Companions
I bumped into your sister Meggie,
and Meggie's always good for a laugh or two,
good to drink grappa in the afternoon.
'What can I say about my dumb sister?'
Meggie said with a laugh and I told her
you didn't understand why I spent a weekend
at a seaside seminar on 'how to meet
people' and on 'the art of speed-dating.'

I told your sister the same ghost story
the married man tells Annabeth Gish
in *Mystic Pizza* and, satisfied with
how that went, her hand grazing my shoulder
as she excused herself, when she got back
I asked, 'Wanna just go and grab something?'
and Meggie said, 'Why stop there, Schlitzy?'
I laughed and asked if she wouldn't call me
by the nickname you gave me last May.
She looked at me, both familiar and strange,
and said, 'I was just thinking of calling you
some dumb, drunk, pasty hick I picked up
in a bar. That or *Punkinhead McGee.*
Which one do you think has a better ring?'
She thought it would be more convenient
if we ordered something from her place;
she bragged about some sketch takeout place
which had 'jumbo tandoori po' boys,'
but we quickly forgot about the subs.
Later, I listened to some of her CDs:
the OST to *Dawson's Creek*, which was
the most beautiful thing I ever heard –
like the tender ache of first love itself.
I said her taste was both 'progressive
and classic.' In the morning, I scooped up
my things and, in Companions again,
set out to finish those poems started
the day before, not fixing on objects,
thinking about you, stung and complaining:
'I guess I just don't understand you.'

Li-Lo (Blazon)

The *Fully Loaded, Freaky Friday* smasher
holed up in rehab but still looking smart.
Taking tittering, blind, tabloid teasers
but smiling right into the camera's heart.
Li-Lo, each freckle a blushed diamond,
rampaging redheaded or raven-tressed,
or at the wheel, weaving, a Valley blond
and always some puss's Hollywood mess.
A look-at-me bandage around her wrist,
her voice a Marlboro-strafed gravel,
and sufficiently Roosevelt Hotel blessed
to say, 'I hate children! I hate them all!'
Humpdays will come and humpdays will go:
La bella vita forever, *bella* Li-Lo.

Summerland

In the future, Kraft Macaroni and Cheese
will become so cheesy we will no longer
know sadness. In a calculated move
to get younger people more interested
in poems, Browning's *Pippa Passes*
will be retitled *Whatevs*. And quite soon,
howevs, the one I'll just call 'Shc' will be
in Myrtle Beach, avoiding the sun.
Nearby the racks of wiffle balls, Speedos,
NASCAR towels and quality fake vomit,
nearby stands for funnel cakes and corn dogs,
by seaside pavilions showcasing bands
most people think broke up in eighties,
she will be indoors (AC to eleven),
working on her novel. There will
be much less downloading Amy Winehouse
songs than before and far much less buying
new pants than most consider a normal
pants-buying regimen. In the future,
it will be determined that Lincoln
greatly suffered from restless-leg syndrome.
We will learn open-face sandwiches
were discovered by Chopin. The future
will be particularly bright for those
who've invested in medicated socks.
Cigarettes will make a spectacular
post-cancer comeback and Philip Morris
will produce a smoke that will last longer
than it takes Neptune to circle the sun,
or however long it takes Sting to have sex.
O Bright! Maybe before she finishes

her novel, all the world will discover
the true evil behind Tom, the generic
MySpace friend (whose hero is Nietzsche).
The pure evil of Tom; the *pure evil*.
With longer lives and warmer sun, the future,
full of happy pectoral muscles,
will see more exciting new combinations
of the words 'Angelina' and 'online.'
In the future there'll be melon-coloured
tombstones and loose-tooth meds that taste
twenty-six per cent less mediciny.
The future will feature some wise choices.
She wouldn't think of having a long novel start
'The idiot's drinking Schlitz Light again,'
because who would want to hear such things?
That doesn't sound like a killer first line –
aren't novels meant to have killer first lines?
The Carolina sun-moments, coming, going,
will, I think, be of little allure to her,
and if she does find some gamesome mood
she certainly packed enough swimwear.
The future will be full of shiny new books
and I promise to skim at least one of them.

Act II.ii

'A hero perish, or a sparrow fall.
Atoms or systems into ruin hurl'd
And now a bubble burst, and now a world.'
                    – Alexander Pope, *An Essay on Man*

Aloha

'Our form is as rigid as a sonnet,'
Jack Lord said about *Hawaii Five-O*.
'I'm as popular as a stuck spinnet,'
I said to a hostile poetry crowd.
Jack Lord's paintings are Post-Impressionist,
the leeward palm trees red in sunrise.
I like old pictures of Ruth St. Denis
and I like sushi when it's chicken fried.
Steve McGarrett had a little helipad
and I've always done well in some events:
the Go-To-Hell-A-Thon, the Shove-It-iad,
the Tournament of I'll-Drown-in-the-Sea,
the I'm Dying (And Soon) Super Bowl.
Super Bowl, Horatio, Super Bowl!

McGarrett

I never liked those poems by Wo Fat,
the ones where he complains about his life
to passively boast of his accomplishments:
'I wasn't / the most popular / student
at Harvard.' 'It took me / a good while
to stop being angry at how / Chairman
Mao / suggested my tennis / needed work.'
'I was most unhappy / with the pictures
of me / in the hardcover edition
of / *Raise High the Banzai Pipeline*.'
Not long after Wo Fat's release from jail,
not long after his subsequent fame
as an author of melancholic poetry
(which allegedly made prison guards cry
and made my name known only on his terms),
I agreed to meet him at Waldenbooks
in the Royal Hawaiian Shopping Center,
where island birds dart about indoors.
I agreed to have coffee with Wo Fat,
to put away the Navy manners
that saw me through my youth and my job,
where I would, sans booze, toast my arch-enemy
and then head out to the North Shore,
past the GI barracks and pineapple fields,
just to hang out in hippie surf shops
and buy seashell leis and dawdle about
the sticky sidewalks of Matsumoto's.
But first, among rows of cheap ukuleles,
I watched the mall birds dart about and waited.
No matter what Wo Fat took from me,
I knew God was soon to take a little more.

Wo Fat could still drive and I could not;
Wo Fat could still read regular type
and I could not; Wo Fat did not wait
for phone calls or visitors but I did.
We were the same age. I took care of myself,
eschewing shooters and horny tourists too,
where Wo Fat smoked Cohibas by dawn light
and took out dancers from hotel hula shows
just to watch him eat a big steak dinner.
But there was no doubt on that strange day
Wo Fat looked younger than me in every way.
After the coffees we drove to Hale'iwa.
He played CDs his daughter had burned
and I didn't recognize a single song.
I may have fallen asleep in the car;
I think he talked about his new book tour,
the hardship of stating his case repeatedly.
We ended up at an impromptu luau,
hot dogs and saimin and girls in grass skirts.
They had put leis together to welcome us.
For Wo Fat, it was a yellow 'Ilima lei,
bright and waxy as a supermarket lemon,
while I was draped in green Limu kala.
Whatever it was I was meant to say,
whatever assassination was meant
to be attempted, ended in decaf.
If there was any punching left in me
you wouldn't know by the way I sat down
and said, 'I'm tired. I've had enough.'
An old lieutenant who shook Wo Fat's hand
agreed to take me back to Honolulu.
In the back of the car, I stared off
at the waxy black volcanic cliffs,

the jungled plumeria, the deep greens
of succulents and tropical produce.
But sunlight was bad for what was left
of my eyes so I likely slept until home.
I would give you all paniolo flowers
for how the evening came on to me;
the hydrangea and forget-me-not collars
to be tossed on the skin of the sea.

Five-O

'Aloha, suckers,' Steve says unto poi
Bring me to Toronto but bring me poi
Certifiably drown'd in an unstirred poi
Dave-o has his dander but I have poi
Every good boy deserves favourable poi
'Friendship's full of dregs' for Timon of Poi
Goodyear Theater Presents: *Time for Poi*
He was a Sk8er poi, said See ya later poi
I'm not thinking of the poetry of poi
Jack in the Box's 'Jack Lord combo' poi
Kono's plastic Oregon coast brand poi
Lono's godhead in a lead spoon of poi
McGarrett holds his pompadour with poi
Next to death we will always have poi
O, we will always have the poor and poi
Phenomenologically day-old poi
Quoting from Poe's 'The Raven,' 'Never poi'
Runner at third, he hit a high poi
Spring books will see my collection *Lardpoi*
Tony says to Angela, 'Poi, eh; eh, poi'
Unctuous, pasty, purple, dirt-flavoured poi
Vince Vaughn comforts Jen with homemade poi
Woe unto Wo Fat's sweet side dish of poi
X-factoring purple vagaries of poi
You know nothing about those who eat poi
Zulu played Kono, seasons one to poi

Infinity

McGarrett slams the wad into the heroin.
McGarrett confronts Wo Fat on the deck.
McGarrett in deep cover as a hippie.
McGarrett says, 'Where's the ego? What's his mark?'
McGarrett takes a secretary out.
McGarrett negotiates surrender.
McGarrett is suddenly in Thailand.
McGarrett seems to appreciate jazz.
McGarrett sent his poems to *Ring Clone*.
McGarrett was stung by their rejection.
McGarrett knows he's bested by Apollo.
McGarrett fucks her in the gas station.
McGarrett's navy tats are most sincere.
McGarrett est saturam non scribere.

Act III

'Couche-toi sans pudeur
Vieux cheval … '

– Baudelaire, 'Le goût de néant'

Breakfast

Another bowl of Corn-Syrup Crunchies,
sweet Sugar-Frosted Tomorrow-o's ...
you can hear Sheryl Crow sing right to you:
'If it makes you happy... you could be dead.'
You flip through the catalogues:
the wristwatch guys with their four-button suits,
eyed by women sipping flavoured coffees,
heading out, with leather case, to the Ave.
Would that case be filled with sweet yellow pills –
Elvis-strength, Elvis-meets-Orpheus strength –
the perfect accessory to smart, snug,
dress-casual at your dread workplace.
Morning in a city you can't love,
and you bus it up, bus it down downtown;
the slog that makes it all go so soggy
when once you stood so iron-fortified,
filled with highly needed riboflavins.
'If your name is Pappy, it can't be Chad;
if your name is Pappy, don't call yourself
Chad.' Syrup Crunchies have you desk-crashing,
impervious to local coffee stands.
Through the years you've developed a rep
as cubicleland's trusty 'trivia guy' –
most likely to know the unlikely name
of some desperate character actor –
when they want to know who played Gitchy-Lou
in *Hey! There's a Husky in My Salon!*
they ask you. Even if on occasion
you scream, 'Joan Fontaine! I can't believe
you don't know who Joan Fontaine is!'
they always ask you. At your desk, you think

of your stint at Buford Business College,
walking away from sure certificate
into the folds of the Bandicoot Pub;
the Bandicoot's nooks still on your mind –
aye, those nooks so nooky with their nookness,
where, nestled, you've often asked, 'If I drink
this whole pint without upchucking
will you go out with me?' Good times, good times.
At work, you feel like a chimp wearing pants.
You take to the phones, trying to coax
credit card numbers from senior citizens,
and you're dreaming of quitting, of quitting,
of uncorking one great big last one: O,
would you walk into your parents' basement
and ride the sofa to oblivion
and feel the fate of the small actor,
the touch of *Coriolanus* he brings
to the role of Second Old Man in the Bank,
the smidge of Willy Loman in his stint
as UPS Guy? Weary steps upstairs.
An answer to your own trivia game.
Stanley Kowalski, meet Blossom's father;
Cyrano, say hello to all the guys
in the ads for 'hair restoration techniques.'
Say, if you were Jonathan Silverman,
star of NBC's flop *The Single Guy*,
what would you recommend after your dodgy
show was cancelled two laughless seasons in?
What would you do? Would you just carry on?
Would you tell yourself, 'Okay, single guy,
get on the stage again, be Mercutio,
audition for spiffy new ad campaigns?
Fight and claw for any part you can get,

be it sitcom, romcom or tragicom?'
Or would you say, '*It's over, Jono,*
close that window because all you'll see
out there is your former best friend's limo
speeding off to the set of his new movie
while your SAG card expires.' To hang on
is the character actor's pudding pie –
you know the face but never quite the name.
He makes a living, is good, lives the life,
but, eventually, he is asked to play
Dorothy's love interest on *The Golden Girls*.
Pucker up. It's time to kiss Bea Arthur.
Pucker up. At lunch you get this gem:
'The difference, you realize, is you're part-time,
a *salesman*. We are members of a firm.'
You don't have too much to say to that one.
Many believe guillotines work because the blade's
so sharp, when it's the blade's heaviness
that does all the work – heavy salaries,
heavy homes, heavy holidays, heavy faith.
If it makes you happy, you must be daft.
No need to try to explain or make friends;
get back home to a new bowl of cereal.
For now, just pop one down and desk-snooze,
you know better than ever what they're like:
like they never felt the hand of Elvis
shake the cherry blossoms loose and hearken to
an early summer so he could freckle
the bare shoulders of women off to work;
like they never thanked Elvis for each new day,
for the crunch on the crust of flax-seed bread,
the pear-flavoured schnapps that holds you at night,
or the wools that warmed children's feet.

Like they couldn't bless Elvis's simple gifts:
the sassafras tea that takes you away,
the snapping turtle's forgotten sharp claws,
the sycamore seeds by your headstone.

TiVolta

Golden Girls have been naughty, Fonzarelli,
Old Christine's got it good for the Fonz,
Dusty's trail to diabetes for the Fonz,
It's like … you know, a dying Fonzarelli,
Hazel, have you met Mr. Fonzarelli?
Alice, c'mon, make a snack for the Fonz,
Timmy, sell Lassie right now to the Fonz,
Everything's Archie and Fonzarelli,
Major Dad but minor poetry, Skippy,
'You again?': that's what you say to Skippy,
La petite vie avec Le Morte d'Arthur,
I dream of Jeannie helping old Arthur,
Far out, space nuts, back to earth for Fonzie,
Enos, because I could not stop for Fonzie.

Montreal

'Montreal winter is like a hundred funerals,'
I said to my new best friend in the world,
'if by a *hundred* one means a *thousand*.'
My new best friend, a sophomore at Dartmouth,
in town to fete Quebec's sweet liquor laws,
took my insight philosophically.
'Whoa, dude,' he said. 'You should love your city
more.' Weekend trips for students languishing
in their worlds of *21 or Over*
is as Montreal as a two-cheeked kiss
or a fistfight in the grand parking lot
of the Place Versailles Mall. Do I not love?
Have I not defended this city right down
to how, here, you can't turn right on red?
Did I not suggest local personalities
Ron Reusch, Mitsou and the Great Antonio
have their faces carved into Mount Royal?
And just this past St. Patrick's Day parade,
the oldest such parade in North America,
did I not welcome the Grand Marshall
to splendid St. Catherine Street by yelling,
'Hey! Sparky! I'm a helicopter! Whoo!'?
It's been a bad year. It's been a bad year;
despite the best efforts of Hannah Montana
and Kelly Ripa to keep us all perky,
despite assurances from know-it-alls
who say Silken Laumann and Catriona LeMay Doan
are actually two different people,
Montreal has limped along with its limp.
Pierre Trudeau and Mordecai Richler are gone,
and somebody said they saw Leonard Cohen

in the Gap, berating a clerk, saying,
'You call this snug-fit?' I've been staying clear
of the Smoked Meat Hut and Chez Rosbif alike.
And the east winds that push refinery smoke
away from the island turn warm with spring.
It's been a while since the last season
of the cursed-but-cute Montreal Expos,
who've moved to somewhere with actual fans,
where they don't boo the national anthem
and they don't call the catcher 'the goalie.'
No more Septembers when our star fielders
are traded to the Yankees or the Sox
for an astigmatic shortstop and a can
of diet soda; no more sweet seasons
for 'Big Beer,' twenty-four ounces of trouble
they sold in the last, most hopeless years.
In the empty grandstands of the Big O
I will read *O* magazine and I will have
a Dr. Phil Moment with the sucker
who sits beside me. I'll make up homespun
sayings that make no sense: *As mad as*
a june bug with a cotton flyswatter,
tired as a hen in a peach orchard
with a june bug sitting in the choir.
I'll not wait for the July moving day
to sing the simple songs of Pom bread
and the *Pain du Pom festival de poésie,*
to say, 'O, the poutine! O, the bagels!
O, bagels stuffed full of poutine!' I will
even finish my stinging reply to
the Toronto writer who suggested
Montreal should be renamed 'Loserton.'
Skilled in both cappuccino and latte,

I will say we deserve something classier,
something along the lines of 'Loserton Heights.'
After all, there's a place just up the street
which claims to have invented 'hot chicken,'
and a place called 'verres sterilisés'
(sterilized glasses) where, coincidentally,
I met my new best friend in the whole world.
His girlfriend, Taffy-Jane, was there with him,
and she was just as philosophical.
A sports therapist who really believes
bums can be motivated to succeed,
she said, 'You should really just try to love
yourself a little more.' I left for home
through the Plateau streets towards
pigeon-grey downtown. The chesterfield.
I should love myself a little more.
I should love myself a little more.
God, I hope she meant that in a sexual way.

Fáilte!

I love St. Patrick's Day. I really do.
It's the only holiday completely
ruined by the music of U2. Sure,
Christmas is ruined a bit by the music
of U2, Easter maybe a bit more;
I'm sure more than one Yom Kippur has felt
less atoneful because of the music
of U2, and, let's face it, every day
is a little ruined by the music
of U2. But Paddy's Day is the only day
completely ruined by the music
of U2. That makes it special among days
and is, actually, an amazing legacy
of Bono's unofficial papacy.

Voice-Over

Scheduled guests on *The Tony Danza Show*
stay at the luxurious downtown Omni,
where one can listen to quivering ghosts
from the prestigious Lowell family
as they passive-aggressively argue
about the 'Roman fate of America.'
Given established public obsessions
with non-Danza-related materials,
guests will be encouraged to cannonball
to their hearts' content in a swimming pool
located on the luxurious rooftop
of the Omni's sister hotel, the Brase,
part of the Epic Inns and Suites chain.
Transportation is provided by Steelrick,
the world's only line of rickshaws made from
one-hundred-per-cent-non-union steel beams.
'For sturdy bridge and tunnel runs it's Steelrick!'
For additional floral arrangements
we consult the Birdman of Paradise,
known for bouquets where leafs stalks are replaced
by miniature nozzles which can emit
a steady stream of Pomposa di Palco,
the new fragrance from the Markoff label,
as well as their line of unique hybrids
such as the Mary Tyler Mayapple,
Mary Tyler Milkweed (Poke Sallet Mary),
and Mary Tyler Monkshood, finely ground
to make a sweet nighty-night medicine
which reminds you of Santa Monica
no matter what tubercular hole you call home.
Members of our studio audience

are given a gift basket from Bookland,
including the hardcover releases
Sade: My Life, Cooking with Gatorade,
and '*I Did Not Have Sex With That Woman*':
The Gettysburg Address for Our Time.
Selling books like there's no tomorrow,
it's Bookland! 1-800-DNTBDMB.
Complimentary digital recordings
of *The Best of the Tony Danza Show*
are provided to all who make it to the end of
each taping, including classic moments
like where Tony sings 'Eye of the Tiger'
to a handful of Hurricane Katrina survivors,
or where Tony repeatedly cries
when reminded of how Emeril Lagasse
turned up his nose at Tony's recipe
for Mrs. Rossini's Turkey Rossignol.
Mr. Danza's wardrobe provided by
Hillker's of the Canyon, makers of fine clothes
and shiny adult-pleasure products since
Major Nelson first had Colonel Bellows
detained for psychiatric observation.
Uno abbondanza di Tony Danza;
audience members will also receive
a fifty-dollar gift certificate
for the newest and best fast-food
restaurant in the country, the Happy Bun.
The Happy Bun, where morbid thoughts
are as unwelcome as unwashed hands,
and if you've felt like you were nothing,
like you've been rejected by society,
even a society of tuneless snoots
who think wincing at your expressed beliefs

is akin to composing *La Bohème*,
you'll lose those feelings at the Happy Bun,
and when this bun-induced bliss fades away,
for one lucky man in the audience
(and, let's be sure, that lucky man is you!),
a creeping sense of emptiness will come
and take over your body and spirit;
you will finally understand no one
will ever, for as long as you shall live,
look up from their wine (taco plate) to say,
'I find myself really attracted to you.'
Upon this sad-but-true revelation,
you will be fitted in stylish Vans shoes
and ushered into the city streets
where you will be constantly ridiculed
about your troglodytic appearance,
so when a few thugs come to wail on you
you will say, 'I am ready, sweet punks,
take out my melon before I have to.'
And when you wake in an upscale hospital,
the aroma of lavender in the soft air,
a trained physician will patiently explain
that your cancer is a stage-five cancer
and, well, stage five is not a good thing.
With a little boost from our dizzy friends
at Golden-Apple Distilleries Inc.,
Rogaine (now in a lemon-lime spray gel),
and a brand new violet iPod Nano,
you will surprise yourself by seeing death
not as a chance to reconcile with God
or to seek meaning in the love you know;
instead, you will shred the last bits of trust
you once thought were the fabric of your life

by deciding to leave Earth in a blaze
of prossie-humping, needle-twiddling debauch.
Suffering severe hallucinations,
you will take to your bed for the last time
and you will try to scratch out a poem.
Don't be surprised if, at this dark moment,
by sheer miracle, an apparition
of your beloved should finally come to you
and she will say, 'Sure, I remember you.
Oh yeah, those lap dances at Cheetah's
were so special. You noted my scarlet
G-string, then my white garter belt,
as if I couldn't tell what colour my outfits
were. How could I forget you, *Professor*?'
Then, after checking her cell for the time,
your beloved will firmly lead you through
the particulars of your farewell piece.
She will suggest you write it directly to her,
as a letter and, to make it easy,
she'll suggest you follow the melody
to the Beach Boys classic 'Wouldn't It Be Nice?'
Mindful of the proximity of death,
she'll make circular gestures with her finger
and you will be carefully reminded
of the difficulty of love and how
no one much likes reading your poetry.
Wouldn't it be nice to fuck in hotels
While our other lives just lingered on?
But then you'd have to read my stupid poems
With images of our secret love.
Tonight you're mine because I'm dreaming:
Let's dream together, let's dream together.

Exodus

Like a good girl, Edith died offstage;
like a good boy, Henry died in a crash.
No one around to see the body droop
from heart clinic to oncology.
In the novel version, Kimmy Gibbler
can articulate the pain of friendlessness;
in the show she wears big, baubly earrings
and cheers her pals on to a life she can't have.
The sitcom version of Sylvia Plath's life,
Sylvia, has the lead being cheery,
her darkness blamed on a mother who smokes
(played gallantly by Valerie Harper).
Someone was talking to Judging Amy
asking, 'Judging Amy, will I live?'
and Judging Amy had to tell the dope,
'Live or die, fool, I am Judging Amy!
Do you ask Judging Amy when you know
Judging Amy did not spare your father
even after you watched him try to eat
hospital yogurt after the surgeons
removed most of his mouth? Kneel before me.
What do you ask of Judging Amy?
Judging Amy will not spare your mother
and has her eyes on you and your daughter,
your friends, your pets, the plant in your office
which you foolishly gave a name to.'

Rejection

Thank you for sending your work to *Tearsea*.
We regret to inform you we have passed
on your poems 'Mr. Met' and 'Bonne!'
While we thought they were funny / topical,
we are looking for poems that bypass
the faddish ephemera of America
and happily land in more timeless quarters.
We are looking for commitment:
poems sturdy as a pioneer
who's spent seven winters in a soddy,
poems as determined as a space probe
sailing towards Neptune's hollow moons,
poems that radicalize the Tory trough
yet still satisfy the Roman epicure.
For example, *Tearsea* is very proud
to have introduced poet Megan Kiels,
whose new collection, *The Yellow Swelters*,
stages etymologic polities
where *jouissance* meets *gravitas* like a kiss
between a suburban blond with barrettes
and Lord Byron perched on a Harley.
Hers is the rarity we most cherish,
not common in the subway-stop lives
of television's constituency,
where it's all *Kelly Clarkson Sings Songs of Hope*
and saving money on bags of Cheetos.
Our Turner Madsen special edition,
which you've undoubtedly read yourself,
further demonstrates the bold standards
Tearsea has set for literary risk:
like Madsen's unforgettable poem

in which paunchy and foul-mouthed golfers trudge
over the grounds of an ancient burial site,
their English curses coming out of bunkers,
their clubs gleaming 'like fixèd bayonets.'
It is true, *Tearsea*'s authors are the best.
Our pages are frequently occupied
by the famed authors of such classics as
*The Feverfew Shop, East of Mud Falls,
Zinna's Charm* and *A Serving of Lenity*.
We're not bragging but note, *bona fide*,
these writers have won, on many occasions,
the country's most prestigious awards,
both the Webscott prize and Adrianna grant,
but we do not put stock in such things –
awards are meaningless to us. *Tearsea*
rejects the language of radio call-ins,
the language of the late-night hipster,
and the language of 'after a few drinks.'
We welcome those who are versed in *progress*,
those who feel the future *depends* on verse,
who compassionately tune lexicons
away from gum-stuck seats in the nosebleeds
so we may finally hear a poem's smack.
We welcome the woman whose mute father
left her to 'voyage between shadows'
and unpin the prose of her oppression;
the bad boy who can't help but sweet-talk,
who sends columbines to his mistresses
and bodyshaves in the complete dark.
Even at its inception, when *Tearsea*
was handmade and called *La Raffinata*,
we wanted only poets of blood and saltcod,
poets of heath-damp ankles and scraped shins,

poets who love the clip-clop-clops of hooves,
poets who believe in their native beauty,
poets who know freedom to eat Burger King
is not freedom but rank servility.
Tired of the gimcrack catachresis,
the meretricious pettifoggery
and farouche intemperability
of kids raised on Gilligan and powdered juice,
we ask poetry to retain its own mien,
and for that, *Tearsea*'s never embarrassed.
We are not just a simple magazine,
but a sherry-high, leather-bound huzzah.
We don't drink 'sodee,' we don't watch 'the tube.'
Sure, there's amusement in some of your lines,
like 'Who will buy my dirty potatoes?'
But does 'Who will buy my dirty potatoes?'
bear repeating a full twenty-two times?
You might want to try a different journal,
maybe one with a more fun philosophy,
one of those tickling little lit-mags
who might love your little quiz-show things.
Do they not burst like bubbles over time?
Or, as *Tearsea*'s Rebecca Plover wrote,
Freed from maple shade and smoked-eel supper,
you gave back to the unswept city square
what advertisements said you must owe.
Thank you for taking the time for *Tearsea*
and good luck placing your work elsewhere.

Redemption

Doesn't Shania capture Leviathan
and convince it to play bass in her band?
Doesn't Shania declaw the ghosts of bears
as they galumph through Ghost-Bear Land?
Shania stood up for you when you fell
into a four-to-five-year-long despair;
Shania thinks it's nice but doesn't mind
if you don't notice how she wears her hair.
She's waiting with you at your MRI,
she's putting a blush of blue in the night sky.
Imagine, O sufferers, the great peace
that comes when Shania touches your head,
when she looks at you and says, 'Take it easy,
Hoss, lie down without embarrassment.'

Manhattan

Two dogs walk into a Manhattan bar,
a fox terrier and an Afghan hound.
The Afghan sits at the bar, orders beer,
stuffs his mouth full of pretzels and says,
'What is it with this place? Why's it so dead?'
The terrier talks of a staff party
upstairs, a 'beautiful people only' affair:
pedicures, mojitos and hands on arms.
'Renée Zellweger left Los Angeles
craving a Gotham *literary party*,
so she'll be happier up there than she was
in her beaded red dress on Oscar night.'
The terrier looks dejected at the thought.
'It's a book launch for a West Side poet,
the one who compares past loves to puffins
and who does not giggle when he describes
an Alaskan species' *tiny erectile horn*.'
He has a shot of Jack, and another,
then recites his own unique poetry:
Glam as a half gram in old Amsterdam
with Jennifer Aniston in the stands
making Kal Kan sands with her own hands –
O, glamorous as old Saint Stammerous
stuttering how he's an upstairs man!
Sensing the terrier's gloom – suspecting
he had a doghouse full of unread things
(novels that compare past loves to warfare,
detailed descriptions of water dishes),
the hound changes subjects, slurping back beer.
He says, 'You know what drink is really tasty?
The fine drink of *leaving*. What's better?

A little sip of *getting the hell out*
rarely fails to satisfy. You with me?'
It's a cold October night in the city;
the garbage collectors have been on strike
and the north winds protect them from the stink.
They end up at a Village cantina,
just for the tall margarita pitchers
and the sad basement-like surroundings,
watching cute kids bone up for Bleecker St.,
one drink away from a *Girls Gone Wild* tape.
But the exclusive party of bookish types
remained on the terrier's mind.
He proposed a MacArthur-like return:
'Look, you can never underestimate
the simple sway of *No Talking Dogs*
and we have to do what we can to fight,
not for us so much, but for all talking dogs –
even the talking cats and talking squirrels
(may they otherwise die) of the future.'
On the way, unable to hail a cab,
the hound talked the terrier out of it,
using metaphors of three-leggedness,
metaphors of Alpo and T-bone steak ...
the wisdom that comes from harsh exclusion.
'What would you do if you had fifty bucks?'
the Hound asked as they tramped all the way
to a quiet Irish bar on 2nd.
'Ever wonder what puffin tastes like?'
the Terrier joked before pulling up a seat,
and, hearing this, the bartender tore in:
'I thought I told you guys last week,
don't come here if you're going to talk
about devouring wildlife, especially

the adorable big-eyed Arctic kind.
It scares the regulars. *Feck!* Write a song
or an off-Broadway thing if you must –
but don't force me to put you to the curb.'

October

Nowadays, I spend my time close to home
and I still have my first computer.
I sleep the way a teenager might: face-
first in the pillow and for twelve hours
straight. I don't want for savings but usually
I'm unhappy. I maintain some confidence
a new job will get me to where I could
buy a nice plot in the same cemetery
where my sister's buried. She's by a yellow
apple tree which drops its fruit in October
(of course) and the floored apples rot until
the snows come. To the edge of her stone
there's a soft patch with bright shamrocks
and plastic roses in a coffee can.

Irresistible

I have always been proud of my powers
of resistance. I've said no to Betamax,
no to acid-wash jeans, no to condos,
no to the finale of *Dancing with the Stars*
and, for years, I've been able to say no
to my sweetheart's ridiculous demands
we watch movies with 'plot and character.'
What's the point? I mean, everybody knows
all good films share one thing in common –
the phrase 'Starring Bruce Lee.' However,
when I was young, it was hard to say no.
Just as the salmon cannot refuse
swimming upstream to spawn, I could not resist
the musical inventions of Blue Oyster Cult
any more than I could resist shoplifting
knock-off track pants in Miracle Mart
or signing high school yearbooks with the phrase
'Rock it like a crazy-armed rocktopus!'
That's the way I thought things were: on a track,
straight to the factories on the horizon
and I would find it impossible not to spend
my whole life in the oil refineries
deep in the east end of Montreal ...
much like my guidance councillor found it
impossible not to laugh when I suggested
I wanted to go to Stanford. Fate ruled me,
and time would just fix me where I was born,
as inevitably as clams end in chowder,
like genie pants fitted on MC Hammer,
like the love between a man and a tractor,
like skipping dessert to Karen Carpenter.

As Danny Bonaduce is fated to the asylum,
as the flunk makes it to sweet flunkydom,
as the skunk skunks up the skunktorium,
as Opie shrunk from Andy's opprobrium.
Somehow, I started writing short stories.
Short stories to keep before I would die.
And, though I grew up in a house of brothers
who all had jobs and construction boots,
I kept to the notion you write what you know.
Hence, all my stories were about dubbin,
a greasy wax used to weather-treat leather –
an essential to preserving good workwear.
Dubbin comes in a puck-shaped tin and smells
like a mix of Lemon Pledge and smoked lard.
So, my first literary efforts went:
'Did you dubbin those boots? Has anyone
seen my dubbin? There's plenty of dubbin.
You did a good job dubbinin' those boots!
Jesus Christ! It smells like dubbin in here!'
It was a humble start on my way
to my most noted achievements in letters:
my hand-printed guide to a better life,
Improve Your Self-Esteem with Yogurt and Gin,
and my petition to get my dormitory
renamed 'Mouth-Sore Hall.' I was uplifted!
Even though I worked the same side of the street
as rich kids who'd been tranformed to *artistes*
and who believed ironically saying
'God Bless America' was the height of sarcasm,
I somehow learned how to say no.
I may have still believed stress was best dealt with
via a mix of steak dinners and punching,
but I no longer just said yes whenever asked.

In *Enter the Dragon*, Bruce Lee rejects
his father's teachings to avenge injustice.
In *Fists of Fury*, Bruce Lee denies
his father's teachings to avenge injustice.
Saying no, esp. to good things,
made me think I could endure life's pains,
even pains otherwise unendurable –
like breaking both legs and both ankles,
or a long car ride with a Tom Waits fan.
When a poet told me he knew suffering
because he suffered from 'imposter syndrome,'
a psychoanalytic term assigned
to those who feel unworthy of any praise,
I never suggested to the poet,
in his case, perhaps 'imposter syndrome'
was better called 'rational conscience.'
Saying no is the illusion of life left
as we all must say, yes, I will die.
Because I could not stop for death he
kindly kicked me with steel toes like Bruce Lee.
Those of us who wrote poems in taverns,
and who thought we would just flailingly die
of ODs in 29th St. apartments,
or being chased by moustached creditors
through the streets of Rabat, or would perish
by a lakeside fire having caught a last trout –
we're dying wholesale of complications
from high blood pressure, fighting cancer
in little hospital rooms calling out
for our mothers and for a cigarette.
To learn the art of fighting without fighting –
knowing death is the only thing irresistible.

Sempervivum

Whether Avril Lavigne makes it or not.
Whether Alanis tops *Jagged Little Pill*.
Whether Céline Dion sells out Caesars.
Whether Nelly Furtado plays what she wants.
Whether Shania sings Timmins to sleep.
Whether Anne Murray's hair ever moves an inch.
Whether k.d. lang craves anonymity.
Whether Skye Sweetnam is ever recognized.
Whether Sarah McLachlan inspires new
generations of women to download
pictures of a much younger Jann Arden,
I will pull over and step into death
like it was a roadside vegetable stand:
Special! Death w/ bag onions: $2.

Sitcom

'Don't forget the knife in my boot,' I'd say
to myself, not even sure what I meant –
autumn yarrow and purple-flowered catmint
on a September street, not far from home.
I couldn't see Venus in the night sky
or keep up with plot lines in *Judging Amy*,
as I avowed not to play life pretty,
say, 'All's fair!' as erstwhile pals drove away
to Cottage Country, their jobs secure.
Around then, I convinced this girl who danced
in a local girlie show under the name
Princess Diana to come up to my place
just to watch TV, to love Sitcomland
in quiet, while friends left 'I'm disappointed'
messages on our phones – ringers turned off.
Half through a promised week-long *Mary* binge
she said she was worried about me.
Curling herself deep into the sofa,
her fingers red from snacking on Twizzlers,
she hated that I was swearing so much.
The Princess said, 'Why not take a long drive,
just by yourself, sort things out.'
'Nothing is hopeless,' she said, not taking
her eyes from the flickering TV screen.
'Except, of course, Murray's love for Mary.'
Out to where tobacco flowers blossom
and cabbage soups last for two months,
to the seat of Murfreeswood County where
Princess Diana's devout, stout father would say,
'If you pay attention, kid, you can smell
the forest fires from a thousand miles away.'

Diana said that's where her 'Cousin Steve'
has some things of hers – *precious little things,*
you know, frayed diaries and charm bracelets –
I could pick up for her on my way back.
I phoned the Princess from a dark road stop,
a place where I'm sure people go missing –
the kind of people who do not rouse
the Sheriff's department's dogs and fog lights.
I felt better when she answered and said,
'Mary is wearing low-rise, white denim,
a wide belt black with large silver-rimmed holes,
nicely complementing the ring-drawn zippers
of her navy blue sweater, also snug.
A fringy sash comes across her waist,
flapping like a horse's tail, her black hair
in traditional early years' bouffe ... Wow!'
I forgot what was bugging me at work
and took more time off in Christiansburg:
played a shoot-'em-up video game
called *Big Buck Hunt* and mistakenly shot a doe,
ate ice cream and saw a county museum
full of old ice skates, papers from the wars,
and headlines from the town's one great scandal –
a man had two wives who looked just the same.
I checked in to a thirty-five-dollar motel,
settled into some *Laverne and Shirley*s.
Like a long demotivational speech,
give me any chance, I'll coffee-break it:
That's my last e-mail bleeping on your screen.
I call those notes illiterate, suckers.
Goodbye! In the night, Rob's on a jury,
entranced by the sexy testimony
of a falsely accused exotic dancer.

On the *Hillbillies*, Miss Chickadee Laverne
delightfully misunderstands Jethro
when he proposes an 'engagement.'
In dark morning, I navigated
the sculpted and sloped gopher mounds
around interstate motels (who knows where!),
into town to where a bleary-eyed barber
offered a choice between three haircuts:
GI Special, Short Crew and Mr. Clean.
At some beach tacos-'n'-gifts store, I bought her
a bikini bottom with the word 'Princess'
embossed in fuschia across the backside.
I darted through waves of big eaters in
cotton shorts, high-tops and black fanny packs,
each one, I'm sure, saying softly to themselves:
Hallelujah for the knife in my boot,
Hallelujah for the knife in my boot –
that's how you'll know I didn't go to Duke.
In the afternoon, in a blood-sugar daze,
AC turned on max, Bud Light by my side,
Lucy is smuggling a cheese on board
and pretending it's a baby; Rerun
is held up seventeen days in Dallas
and Wally celebrates his decision
to stop telling harmless little white lies
by declaring he's 'earned an indulgence.'
Sabrina maxes out her credit cards
for shoes she'll throw out of a moving car.
Carol Seaver, tired of her girlfriends
talking about how cute her brother is,
moves into a hollowed scarlet oak
to raise falcons which retrieve handguns.
Sister Bertrille, to cool off her attraction

to Carlos, takes advanced Latin lessons
but ends up having sex with her Latin
instructor anyway. *Nunc est bibendum* …
Darrin fidgets in fear of doctors and whores
and Joey Gladstone imitates the patter
of his long-lost mentor, Dr. Miracle.
Dr. Miracle narrates the Eighth Labour
of Hercules: feeding Diomedes
to flesh-eating horses just to tame them,
the horses singing 'Blinded by the Light,'
the horses mumbling out the troubling line,
'Wracked up like a douche in a rumblin' night'?
In part two, Dr. Miracle feels bad,
regrets getting so many things so wrong:
'Like an accent you leave in the bayou,
it can still creep up in the lecture hall.'
'Don't forget the knife in your boot,' Di said,
wondering if I 'even cared a bit,'
saying if I loved her I'd do her one solid –
visit her cousin Steve six hours nearby.
The cousin had her 'frilly-frilly things'
tucked in a few vinyl airline bags,
and a small collection of magazines
and paperbacks that made her mother cry.
I didn't ask if I got a call from work,
I just let the Princess go on and on.
Once I agreed, she talked of the marathon:
'Mary is wearing a brown pleated skirt,
a short-sleeved white tricot tunic;
ever the master of accessorizing,
she has a brown leather belt, clasped
at her waist, showing off her thinness,
and calf-high cream-coloured vinyl boots.

Dressed for a Minneapolis winter,
she puts over a brown suede winter coat
with faux rabbit trim at cuffs and collars.'
I rumbled through mountains and river valleys,
a western stretch that was, apparently,
as close to Pittsburgh as it was to Richmond.
Her cousin Steve tended a small greenhouse
where he grew his own taro for his own poi.
I could tell by his smile, like an indulgent priest,
there was no chance he was the Princess's cousin.
More like an old boyfriend or country pimp.
He smoked as he talked *anthers* and *stigmas*,
he sneered at me with obvious contempt,
talking of 'the soft curl of strychnine trees,
like snakes who've long been anaesthetized;
like the knotty snarls of a begonia shoot.'
His ziplocked bags of frozen homemade poi
he said were laced with antidepressants,
and when I told him I was there for her things,
he said he could use a bowl right away.
He told me to take some from the freezer.
I followed his orders quite carefully,
laying a purple bag in the microwave:
rotate, thaw. I looked at it spin inside.
'Tell the Princess this is from me,' he said
as he stuck a knife into my right side.
I don't know if there was blood on the floor,
but I walked to my car, my head held up,
as if he had said something offensive
at a dinner party I found boring.
'You better run! You tell her that's from me!'
Who knows how long the car ride went on
through pea fields and dusty two-lane highways.

Slumped, near gone, at a deserted rest stop,
I phoned the number just to be familiar,
and just to be familiar she said,
'Mary is living in the high-rise now;
her hair is much lighter, blunt and brassy;
she favours earth tones, beige and umber,
monochromatic pantsuits, tighter tops.
Still the genius with the little glamour touch –
big silver bracelets, beaded necklaces –
there's more of a sense of sad old maid now.
She's alone in a luxury condominium,
but she cooks herself liver and onions
and wears these department-store scarves,
her only concession to blues and whites.
It is a less happy passage in time.
Even Murray is wearing denim suits,
those seventies thigh-length safari jackets.
Even Murray acts like he's still alive.'

Acknowledgements

' … three red halves of starved winter-pears,
Or treat of radishes in April!'
  – Robert Browning, 'How it Strikes A Contemporary'

Some of these poems originally appeared, or will appear, some in different forms, in the following venues: *Career Suicide: Contemporary Literary Humour*, CBC *Poetry Face-Off*, *Damn the Caesars*, *Definitely Not the Opera*, *Five-Oios*, *Future Present*, *Jacket*, *Macaronico*, *Matrix*, *New American Writing*, *The Original Canadian City Dweller's Almanac*, *Palimpsest*, *Texas Review* and the *White Wall Review*. The poems '*Susan #42*' and '*Susan #43*' are very loosely based on two specific episodes of the sitcom *Suddenly Susan*, which were written, respectively, by Becky Hartman Edwards and Andrew Green. The perorations of 'Summerland' are extrapolated from the start of Browning's *Pippa Passes*. The nonsense ending of 'McGarrett' is based on a most sensible line from Juvenal's *Satire I*. The poem 'Timon' is based on a soliloquy from *Timon of Athens* 4.1.1-41.

Thanks to Coach House Books: to Alana Wilcox for her most inspiring care, and to Kevin Connolly, my editor, for his great insight and valued encouragements.

Special notes of gratitude are owed to Jason Camlot and Alessandro Porco, who read many of these poems as they tenuously started (as email attachments) and who always helped with good humour and collegial respect. Above and beyond thanks to Lynn Crosbie, whose amazing friendship and knowledge of poetry was, as always, my most reliable light.

Thanks to Arjun Basu, Paul Beer, Mary Crosbie, Jim Crosbie, John Fraser, Jon Paul Fiorentino, Gary Hillier, Anastasia Jones, Nick Lolordo, Scott Macdonald, Nick and Bernadette Mount, Sara Peters, Matthew Rosenberg, Adam Steinberg, Todd Swift, Erin Vollick and Adrienne Weiss. To Rob Allen, in memoriam. To Carol, sweet sunshine. To my wonderful parents, John and Mary, my sister Janice, my brother Johnny, and my partner in crime, my brother Mike.

About the Author

David McGimpsey was born and raised in Montreal. He has a Ph.D. in English literature and he currently teaches creative writing at Concordia University. He is the author of several collections of poetry, a book of fiction and a critical monograph on the subject of baseball and American culture. David plays guitar and sings in the rock band Puggy Hammer and has also performed as a stand-up comedian. His travel writings appear frequently in the *Globe and Mail* and he writes a regular column about sandwiches for *EnRoute* magazine.

Other books by David McGimpsey

Poetry
Dogboy
Lardcake
Hamburger Valley, California

Fiction
Certifiable

Non-fiction
Imagining Baseball: America's Pastime and Popular Culture

Typeset in Goudy Sans and Sabon Next
Printed and bound at the Coach House on
bpNichol Lane

Edited for the press by Kevin Connolly
Designed by Alana Wilcox

Coach House Books
401 Huron St. on bpNichol Lane
Toronto, Ontario M 5 S 2G 5

800 367 6360
416 979 2217

mail@chbooks.com
www.chbooks.com